Stori

MW00915055

Fun and Inspirational Short Stories of Dogs and Their Parents

Storiesoftails.com

Chandler Jeffries

BELLA MEDIA PUBLISHING

Copyright 2013 Bella Media Publishing
BellaMediaPublishing.com

What Readers Are Saying ...

"So Cute – Great Read... You need this book, just because..." –
Maya Sheppard

"Must read for dog lovers!" – Jason Renschler

"...touching and adorable...the best stories...all in one place." –
Sean

*"Wonderful, Heartwarming Stories...a must read for any
animal lover"* – Lori Loudon

This book contains material protected under International and Federal Copyright laws and Treaties. Any unauthorized reprint or use of this material is prohibited.

Unauthorized duplication or distribution of this material in any form is strictly prohibited. Violators will be prosecuted to the fullest extent of the law.

No part of this publication may be reproduced, stored in a retrieval system or transmitted in any form or by any means, electronic, mechanical, photocopying, recording or otherwise, without prior written permission from the author/publisher.

The author, publisher, and distributor of this product assume no responsibility for the use or misuse of this product, or for any physical or mental injury, damage and/or financial loss sustained to persons or property as a result of using this system. The liability, negligence, use, misuse or abuse of the operation of any methods, strategies, instructions or ideas contained in the material herein is the sole responsibility of the reader.

The material contained in this publication is provided for information purposes only!

Version 2013.9.6

Chandler Jeffries

Chandler Jeffries is a Best Selling Author and experienced dog trainer that enjoys working with families and their children to train their dogs. He's the owner of **WellBehavedIn14Days.com.**

Twitter
http://twitter.com/chandlerjeffrie

Facebook
http://facebook.com/chandlerjeffriesfan

Other Books by Chandler Jeffries

14 Days to a Well-Behaved Dog

Table of Contents

Introduction

Throughout my travels I've come across hundreds and hundreds of people that have touching, profound and humorous stories of their dogs. I often find myself repeating them to my friends, family and clients and they always seem to bring a smile, laugh and occasional tear to their eyes.

The short stories contained in this book were contributed and written by them. Enjoy these stories and may they bring happiness to your life as they did mine.

Remember to always love your dog. All they want is your love and care.

- Chandler Jeffries

Sometimes Size Doesn't Matter

Jessica Blaine

When I was a little girl growing up in Kingsport, Tennessee I was around animals a lot. My mom, dad and I lived in the same house as my grandparents on a farm at the end of a dirt road. The farm wasn't much really, just a pretty large garden and a few extra hills where my grandfather, everyone called him Pa, raised some potatoes, corn, and tobacco. The potatoes and tobacco were cash crops that were sold for extra money to some wholesalers in town and occasionally from Pa's truck on the side of the road. We had a few milk cows on the farm, some dairy goats that also got milked, and some chickens for fresh eggs.

From the time I was six or seven years old I helped with the animals and loved them all. Even so, there was one thing I wanted more than anything else in the whole world, a puppy. The problem was that the way Pa and my dad thought about dogs was not my way. They thought of dogs as working animals. They were either there to guard the chickens, goats and other livestock, or they were hunting dogs like Pa's retriever, Buddy. What I wanted, though, was a friend.

Living at the end of Morris Road in an isolated spot called Cole Holler meant there were no kids my age within easy walking distance. Sure, I had friends at school, and during the school year I looked forward to the bumpy ride on the old yellow bus with Mr. Ivory, our bus driver. I'd spend the day with other kids at school, but when I got home, it was just me and Ma and Pa most days. I was pretty lonely. My Mom and Dad were working in Kingsport and were gone a lot back then.

I'd asked for a puppy every Christmas as far back as I could recall, but when I looked under the tree on Christmas morning I never found what I was looking for. I always got the explanation that Santa couldn't bring a little puppy on a flying sled in Winter, so maybe in the Spring I'd get one for my birthday. I don't really recall what the explanation was on my birthday, but I do know that no puppy was forthcoming for several years despite my begging. As awful as the waiting and disappointment had seemed to my little girl self, when I turned eleven things changed.

My Mom and Dad were getting ready to move from Kingsport to Chicago for better jobs. Since nothing was locked in yet and they would be staying with relatives, I was to remain in Kingsport with Ma and Pa. The big move of my parents was taking place the day after my eleventh birthday. True to form I once again made the pitch for a puppy but got silence from my Dad and a nervous glance from my Mom. I decided that was a bad omen. It looked like no puppy once again. Maybe it was guilt that they were leaving me there with my grandparents, but when I woke up on birthday, my Dad was sitting on the side of my bed.

"Wake up sleepyhead, happy eleventh birthday...time to go pick out a puppy." Dad said.

Dad and I drove down to the animal shelter and after we signed in we walked along a row of pens with all kind of dogs in them. Dad kept encouraging me to get one of the setters, retrievers, or mutts that looked like they were going to be big and useful like Buddy. None of those dogs were what I was looking for. Then I saw him. A little puppy all curled up on a dirty blanket. I knew he was the one.

"I want that one, Dad." My Dad skeptically looked in the cage. "Honey, that is some kind of a Daschund mix. He won't get any bigger than nothing."

"He's the one I want," I said.

Dad, to his credit, didn't say anything else. He just paid the fees and thirty minutes later I was riding home with my new puppy.

When we got home my dad asked, "So what are you gonna name him?"

"Arf," I said.

My Dad's eyebrows went up. "Arf?"

I nodded and went into the house. I named my puppy Arf, because I thought it would be funny to stand on the front porch and call him by shouting, "Arf, Arf, Arf!"

That was my sense of humor. All that Summer Arf and I had fun playing around the farm, but Pa and Ma didn't particularly think Arf was all that great. Pa especially thought my puppy was just a waste of food. "He's just a permanent runt," Pa said.

In September I started back to school and Arf would spend the day sleeping on the back porch while Ma worked in the kitchen or hung laundry out on the clothesline. Pa was generally doing something in the barn or out in the fields. My Mom and Dad were still in Chicago working.

One day just after I'd gotten home I heard my Grandmother yelling in the back yard. She'd been out hanging laundry a when a mangy Cocker Spaniel mix had slunk into the yard. He belonged to the people down the road and he was always running wild. Now he found his way around the side of our house near the chicken coop.

Ma figured that the dog was after one of the chickens. By the time she came around the side of the house yelling at the dog, the Cocker Spaniel had knocked one of the chickens down and was trying to kill it. Ma, intent on running the dog off, ran towards it yelling and cursing. But instead of running away the Cocker Spaniel turned on her. His fur came up and he lowered his head, growling threateningly. Ma froze.

Hearing the commotion I had run downstairs and rounded the corner of the house taking in the scene. Immediately understanding this wasn't a good situation, I became worried. Arf had been on the back porch napping. Suddenly, out of the corner of my eye I saw a little brown streak charge around the far side of the house and head directly for the growling Cocker Spaniel at high speed. The invading dog was watching Ma and didn't see Arf making his Kamikaze run.

My heart was pounding and I couldn't move. Arf came in at an acute angle and hit the Spaniel's left rear leg down by the ankle, sinking his little sharp eight month old puppy teeth into the much larger dog's leg as hard as he could. The Spaniel, intent on my Grandmother, didn't know what had just hit him from behind. He yelped and went down with Arf still latched onto his hind leg.

Ma screamed. I screamed. The Spaniel yelped again and started scrambling towards the gate, intent on escape from whatever had just attacked him from behind. The slightly wounded chicken took this opportunity to flee, managing to get airborne for about thirty feet and landing in the low branches of a tree in the yard.

Arf hung onto the Spaniel's leg until the dog managed to kick free of the little terror as he was escaped up the gravel driveway towards the road. I watched as Arf went flying, doing three or four barrel rolls before coming to rest in Ma's blooming Asters.

I had just started towards the purple and white Asters thinking my puppy was dead when he emerged from the flower bed and trotted up to the porch. He started lapping water from his bowl as if this was something that happened every day. I looked at Ma. She was standing where she'd stopped when the Spaniel started growling at her. She shook her head. "Pa will never believe this."

But he did believe it, and from that moment on he never said Arf was just a waste of food or a runt. Every now and then we saw the Spaniel wandering up and down the road. I can't be sure, but when he passed our property it seemed like he moved a little bit faster and glanced around nervously. He never came in our yard again, though.

The Little Bear

Jon Wilcox

I always try to remind myself to take a moment each day to reflect just how precious life can be and just how fast time goes by. Before I knew it my little girl was a teenager. The years had flown by and now, just as she had changed my life so many years ago, it was about to change again.

I can remember the day she was born. It was such an exciting event. There were so many friends and family, and strangers there. People were whizzing about the room trying to keep things clean and organized among the chaos.

She was so small, but so cute. Thinking back to that day makes me smile. She just about fit into the palm of my hand. Her pink skin was warm with just a touch of brown hair. Her little pink nose twitched and her little tiny cry was so adorable.

The moment I laid eyes on her I knew she was mine. I quickly counted to make sure the parts were all there. Ears? Yep. Feet? Yep. Tail? Yep.

There she was, my little Labrador Retriever. It seems like just yesterday she was born and just yesterday she turned my world into a bit of a mess.

Herschy loved to eat everything she shouldn't. From the first day I brought her home she consumed everything. Wooden chairs, window sills, socks, sponges, rugs.

It took a full five years for her to fully calm down and lose the puppy in her. It actually seemed to happen over night and I'm sure the timing was no coincidence.

Miraculously, the day my daughter Nikki came home from the hospital Herschy took notice and became a whole new dog, but she still loved to chew and steal things on occasion.

She attentively watched as the new baby cried, followed as she was carried from room to room and even slept at the doorway to keep watch over her.

I never trained her to do this, it seemed to be instinctive. Herschy became my daughter's keeper, friend and watch dog.

Herschy loved to tease Nikki by stealing her little bear and carrying it around proudly until we had to pry it from her mouth. She never chewed on it, just carried it around. It was definitely a little game to her.

As the years went by Herschy was there every step of the way. As Nikki took her first steps Herschy was right next to her to hold her up. When Nikki fell, Herschy was there to break her fall. The two were inseparable.

Herschy endured years of being dressed up in doll clothes, playing the giant monster that scared away Nikki's dolls and even the enormous horse that would carry her stuffed animals around the house on a make-shift saddle.

As much trouble as Herschy was as a puppy, she more than made up for it by being the best friend and sister to Nikki and really, my other daughter.

When things were stressful for me, or Nikki was unhappy, Herschy became our therapist, listening to our problems and understandingly nodding. She never offered advice other than a caring kiss on the cheek, but we always felt better because of her attention. She seemed to truly understand what it was we needed and at the right moment.

Life in our house always included Herschy and she was welcomed everywhere. And every chance she got, she would steal that little bear and carry it around.

Nikki and I sat in the waiting room waiting to hear from the doctor. Just a few hours before, Herschy refused to stand up or move. Each time we tried to help her she yelped. I felt helpless, worthless and didn't know what to do.

I managed to get the courage and strength to gently wrap her in a blanket and carry her to the car. Nikki and I raced to the vet and here we sat.

When Dr. David finally came to speak my heart sank in fear of the worst. And it was.

Nothing was broken, but something wasn't right in her stomach and they would need to perform surgery the next morning.

Nikki and I were devastated, but we both tried to remain strong for each other. Together we went back to comfort Herschy, say goodnight and do the best we could to remain positive.

That night Nikki and I spent the evening looking through old photos and videos. Everywhere we looked there was Herschy, the center of attention. We spent hours pouring through pictures and laughing. We thought about the first thing we wanted to do with Herschy when she returned home.

In Nikki's caring way, she fluffed Herschy's bed, laid out her toys, put fresh water in her bowl and anxiously waited for the next day when she would return home after school to be greeted by her best friend.

It was 8 am the next day when I received a phone call from the vet. I had anticipated getting a call with an update and had already begun thinking what time I'd need to leave work to pick Herschy up.

My heart sank when then vet told me that Herschy didn't make it through the night. She had seemed perfectly fine when they left that evening.

My eyes filled with tears as I had thought about Herschy laying there alone and quickly my heart stopped as I imagined myself having to break the news to Nikki. I felt terrible.

Dr. David quickly snapped me back to the moment as he asked how I would like to make arrangements for Herschy. As I listened to my options my head spun. Suddenly there was a pause, followed by a very difficult question.

"Will you be coming to pick up the blanket and stuffed bear or would you like to leave those with Herschy?" he asked.

I smiled. Somehow that stuffed bear managed to find its way to Herschy. I felt relief. After all, Herschy wasn't alone last night. She had her bear with her and I know she's now carrying it proudly.

Whisper Buddha

Alan Davidson

"40 Mile-an-Hour Greyhound, Prize Winning Athlete, and Canine Incarnation of Buddha Himself, Dies in Houston, Texas"

Whisper, my fourteen-year-old friend and canine-other for the last nine years, died this morning in my hands. I'm reminded, as I often am when an animal friend dies, of a story by a small town vet:

Belker was a ten year old Blue Heeler, much loved by his owners and their four year old son. Belker had cancer and there was no miracle to save him. The local vet made arrangements to come to their home and euthanize Belker.

The owners wanted Shane, their son, to witness putting Belker to sleep. Maybe he could learn something.

Shane seemed so calm, petting the old dog for the last time, that they wondered if he understood what was going on.

Within a few minutes, Belker slipped peacefully away. The little boy seemed to accept Belker's death without any difficulty or confusion. They sat together for awhile, wondering aloud about the sad fact that animal lives are shorter than human lives.

Shane, who had been listening quietly piped up, "I know why."

Startled, they all turned to him. What came out of his mouth next stunned them – They'd never heard a more comforting explanation.

Shane said, "Everybody is born so that they can learn how to live a good life – like loving everybody and being nice, right?"

The four-year-old continued, "Well, animals already know how to do that, so they don't have to stay as long."

Whisper had mastered "Loving everybody and being nice" long before I met him. He was his name sake, quiet as a Whisper. I can count on two hands the times I heard him bark. But he could give a look that spoke a thousand barks, and launched more than one trip to the dog house for me.

He was dignity incarnate, a bit timid, and wise beyond knowing. I and everyone who knew him–loved him.

The voice told me to adopt a greyhound.

I sometimes get messages inside my head. Shocked at the directive to adopt a dog (at the time I thought of my self as a cat person), I found myself at Greyhound Pets of America Houston looking for a retired racer.

I'd already seen several beautiful dogs I liked, when I asked to meet five-year-old Whisper.

Immediately out of his cage–he ran lickety-split down the long row of the kennels to throw his lanky black body up to look out a port-hole window. A minute later he turned and ran full speed right at me; hurled his front paws to my shoulders and looked me in the eye. I knew Whisper was a sign from the gods and, that day, we became a family.

During our long walks up and down prestigious North and South Boulevards, people stopped to admire his elegant good looks: dark black fur with a blazing white star on his chest, short white socks on his feet, and a soft white tip to his whipping long tail. In winter we'd tromp through Herman Park, where he strutted-his-stuff in a black fleece jacket and long black leash. Whisper stopped traffic everywhere we went.

He was his most handsome when he met a new dog friend. He'd stand stock still, chest held high. His long ears pointing straight up and his equally long tail arching back and up. What a striking, handsome dog he was.

Whisper was soon going to work with me. He'd curl up on his bed in the corner of my massage room. Some clients came to see him as much as me. He was so serene, still and quiet. I called him my Buddha dog. Peace just seemed to flow from him. When I was agitated, he'd nuzzle me with his cold long snout and remind me to pet him...and to chill.

Whisper's greatest gift to me was his knack for just being. When I took the time to study him I was impressed by how easy it was for him to BE his true self. A dog that walked, ran, and slept when he wanted to; a friend who showed kindness and care when I needed it most; a being who demanded I tear my focus away from my selfish-self and pay attention to something, anything else-HIM, usually. He taught me responsibility-the basic art of doing what needed to be done. Walk him. Feed him. Love him. Even when my ego preferred to indulge my self-absorption, Whisper taught me, "It's not all about me. It's about all of us, other people, our animal friends, and the sky/earth song around us."

My first Koan, the Japanese Zen cosmic riddle, asks, "Does a dog have Buddha nature?" My mind will never grasp the answer. But my Big Heart just has to remember Whisper, a master of being his true/unique self, to know, "Yes!" Dogs, as all things, have Buddha nature. Being (Wu) is being. It's everywhere I am conscious. Every time I'm BEING my true self, I'm Whisper, I'm Big Mind, I'm Buddha nature.

Whisper's legs had gotten shaky and his hips pretty weak these last few years. He'd already lived a couple of years past the life expectancy for a big dog and a retired racer.

I like to think all those years of sleeping at the foot of my massage table, or curled up next to me while we meditated, kept him healthy and whole.

Yesterday he slipped in the kitchen and he couldn't get up. His back legs wouldn't hold him. Jim, my husband, and I had to carry him outside. He'd walk a few tottering steps, stop, and cautiously move on, or fall down…there was no way to know. I spent a lot of the night (and morning) on the floor next to him.

I held him, petted him, and thanked him for all the many gifts of friendship he'd given me. At the vet's Whisper seemed serene to his fate. There was nothing else to be done for him. Leg shaved and the port in place he rested, alert, head up, ears at attention, eyes wise and comforting. I held his long snout in my palms as Dr. Michelle pumped the gentle death into his vein. He gave us each a last look, closed his eyes, and died.

Moments later I let his head rest on the pallet. In death he looked elegant, as always; he had a gorgeous way of curling up, his long body a graceful line, his ears surprisingly still at attention.

Whisper had one more gift for me. I felt the shell I've carefully constructed to protect my Big Heart, breaking open-wide open. As I surrendered to the immensity of our friendship together, I cried. I trusted the pain I felt just as I trusted my opening heart.

He was true and giving, as always, up to his very end. Thank you, Whisper, my teacher, my Buddha friend.

They Offer Love, They Ask for Love

Nicole Lee

The love of my life is Ruby. She drools when she sleeps, has a long snout and likes to chew electrical wires, which has given me enough frustrations to write an entire book series on. But despite all of that, I love her.

She has taught me so many lessons about patience and acceptance. Often, she teaches in the midst of horrible situations. Horrible to me, at least.

One particular instance that I will never forget is the day she ran away.

Ruby was two years old, and a typical rebellious teenager. She wouldn't come when called, she liked to jump on the bed and her favorite pastime was to pine after the little boy dog down the street.

She had been tied in the backyard for less than half an hour. I had gone outside to check on her, and lo and behold, she was gone. My only clue was a chewed leash attached to a stake in the ground.

I sighed, grabbed my keys and jumped in the car, like any good parent would.

It was garbage night.

When I saw the first ripped bag, trash strewn across the street, I immediately knew who the culprit was. Furious and embarrassed, I followed her trail for what seemed like miles.

It led me through the suburban roads of my community and down a tiny side street, where I found an old woman sitting on the grass of her overgrown yard. In her lap was Ruby, sleeping peacefully and far too big to fit.

I let out a whoosh of relief and ran out of the car.

"Thank you so much! I am so sorry!" I exclaimed to the woman, who just smiled up at me.

Her name was Margaret and she had been gardening when Ruby whizzed by. Since Ruby was dragging a long piece of her leash, she had been relatively easy to catch.

Margaret invited me in for a cup of coffee and I discovered that she was a sweet, though somewhat lonely, person. It felt good to talk with her and keep her company. Ruby napped at our feet, the little devil!

To this day, I believe that Ruby led me to that particular house. Margaret lives in a nursing home now, and she loves when I bring Ruby to visit! Her husband passed away years ago and her children live out-of-state, so visitors are a special treat.

The two have a beautiful bond, and it only serves to remind me that animals are God's greatest creations. They bring so much warmth, joy and lightheartedness. Dogs don't plot, plan and manipulate others, like their two-legged counterparts.

All they offer is love, and all they ask for in return is love.

This sounds so cliché, but it's true: If human beings were that simple, the world would be beautiful. We can learn so much from our animal companions, and I blessed to have the very best wet-nosed friend ever. Her name is Ruby, and she is the love of my life.

The Only Thing I'd Ever Wanted

Chris Jackson

I can remember the Summer between 6th and 7th grade so clearly. The oldest of three very active and engaged children, I yearned for a pet to call my own. There was always some reason why it wouldn't be so. Allergies that run in the family, too many activities to have the time, or cost of the supplies and veterinary care necessary for good care all precluded me from "the only thing I ever wanted". I begged and pleaded and bargained and reminded both my parents, both when they were together and in those little separate moments that I thought gave me an advantage with the divide and conquer tactics.

I drew pictures of dogs, cut apart magazines with animals in them, and drooled over television commercials in which kids were rolling around with the fluffiest puppies and kittens imaginable.

My parents seemed so dead-set against it and I eventually had given up. Believe me, I didn't want one any less, just didn't feel like anything I tried to argue was causing them to reconsider. There were softball games to focus on, band practice to attend, and little brothers to chase around. So, you can imagine the stir when in between games of a softball tournament, my little brothers were cuddling with someone's little black fur ball of a black lab. He was maybe five pounds, definitely the runt of the litter. He could just barely bounce through the grass of the park, and was barking incessantly at everything and everyone.

"Wouldn't you just love to have one of those?"my dad asked me as I watched the puppy trip himself and roll into a ball.

What a cruel joke! Of course I did. I'd pretty much been talking about nothing else for a month, which is eternity in the attention span of a middle school kid. I was upset enough about his teasing that I didn't even ask who the thing belonged to. I was so upset, I hit a triple that next game, mostly out of pure anger.

I figured whomever had been walking the puppy through the park would be long gone by the end of my game. My brothers would be back to complaining about being bored, and I wouldn't have to worry about being aggravated again over the puppy who'd never be mine.

Wrong again! He was still out there, cute as ever, with my brothers were still chasing him around. Even worse, my dad still had that smug little look on his face that I was sure was the innate parental feeling of glee at their child's dismay. He even had the audacity to bring him up to me and put the now-sleeping baby in my softball glove. Yes, he fit entirely in my softball glove.

Salt rubbed in the wound, my father asked me yet again, "Isn't he just precious? He'd make such a good pet for someone!". I'm sure I could have won eye-rolling contests at this point. I started to push the dog back to my dad, getting more and more upset and wanting to avoid tears. Passed the anger, I was tired and hot and just sad. My dad wouldn't take him back, saying "No, hold onto him a bit longer. I'm talking." So I looked around for the child or parent who was lending him for this humiliating charade. I noticed that very few people were left at the park. In fact, it was just us and two other families.

Starting to get confused, I asked my dad who the puppy belonged to. "Oh, you," he said. "Funny, Dad", I thought to myself.. He said goodbye to the parent he was talking to and we started to walk to the car. I asked him again what I was supposed to do with this dog who clearly belonged to someone else. I'm sure he could sense my annoyance at this point. Holding this little guy just wasn't enough. Dad took the dog from me and opened the front door of his car. In the car was a kennel, new bags of dog food, and all the other items one would purchase after acquiring a new dog.

The tears I had worried about before came. That fat little uncoordinated furry little perfect piece of puppy was coming home with me. It took weeks for it to really sink in that he was staying. I slept next to his crate with him for a week in so he wouldn't be lonely. I bathed him and brushed him and taught him to sit. He's still my best buddy, even though I don't live at home anymore. He's slower now, almost thirteen years old, but still just as much a part of the family as he was that first night. My love for him opened the door to the love of all animals, and my eye-rolling at my Dad has never stopped.

Furry Angel

Mike Harris

It was 5:30 on what I was trying to make a lazy Saturday morning and as usual, more reliable than an alarm clock, there was that tongue slapping me in the face. Buddy, my very loving, goofy and very strong 120lb Pitbull that I had rescued from a shelter two years before. It was an easy choice, I knew the moment I saw him in that cage, he was meant for me. He wasn't big enough to fill both hands but the emotion in his bright blue eyes when they met mine was inescapable. It's fair to say he had me wrapped from the first lick. I had to have him and he's been my shadow ever since.

Some people describe their dogs as children or family members and Buddy is no different. He's been my wingman since day one, and quite successfully I might add. It's a crazy kind of magic cute puppies have on women. Yep, it's safe to say he's my best friend and after this particular morning, a furry angel.

"Come on Buddy, let me sleep". I didn't HAVE to get up before daylight today and by God I wasn't going to, even if it meant buddy peeing in the corner of my room, his favorite spot when I failed to let him out. After another twenty minutes of licking now accompanied by barking, I decided I should just get up, God knows I wasn't getting any more sleep.

"Damn Buddy!" Apparently he was tired of the corner and decided right beside my bed would be a better place. Looking back, it should have been a sign that it just wasn't going to be a 'normal' day. As I was washing my feet I could hear him in the living room jumping on the couch and barking. It was an odd bark, not his usual playful bark.

By the time I made it to the living room buddy was scratching on the wall and just going crazy. I had never seen him like this and couldn't get him to stop. I scolded him but when that failed I opened the door to see if he wanted out. The second I opened the door he darted past me and straight to my neighbor's door where he began scratching and barking again.

My neighbor Frank was a 79 year old retiree from Michigan. His wife had died the previous year and he would often come over for a beer and small talk. I felt bad for him, I knew he was lonely and didn't mind at all canceling poker night from time to time to throw a steak on the grill with my buddy Frank. I thought maybe my neighbor Frank's Golden Retriever ,Missy, was in heat and Buddy just wanted to visit. "Buddy!" I yelled. "Get over here!" he just ignored me and kept on scratching like he was going to scratch right through the door. He would have if I had let him continue. I grabbed his collar and pulled him back. I managed to get him back into the apartment.

I could hear Missy barking next door and I just hoped that she didn't wake up Frank. After another ten minutes or so of listening to Buddy and Missy barking, I started to think something might be wrong.

Frank would never let Missy bark this long, or this early. I hadn't heard him scolding her or go out to get his paper. The walls in the apartment were paper thin. Nothing was sacred or secret between neighbors, which I didn't realize until I went out to get coffee one morning. Frank was there with a wink and a "way to go tiger". Only after I walked back in my room and gave my female guest her coffee did I realize what he was talking about.

Frank wasn't the earliest of risers and I didn't want to wake him up but by this point I was getting nervous, so I went next door and knocked.

After three knocks and no answer I was even more nervous so I ran around to the back door. It was a glass sliding door and I could see in. Frank was sprawled out on the floor and not moving.

I forced the door open and hollered his name as I ran to him. He was face down so I flipped him over to check his breathing and pulse. At the same time I grabbed my phone from my pocket and dialed 911. Frank was alive, but I didn't know how bad it really was. It took about fifteen minutes for the EMS to get there, which seemed like an eternity. I stepped back and let them work, praying they were successful. I wasn't ready to lose my drinking buddy.

About five minutes later they had him on a gurney and wheeled him out to the ambulance. I walked beside him talking and holding his hand, hoping he could hear me. I told him he wasn't allowed to go anywhere and I'd have a beer and a steak waiting for him when he got back.

Now I'm not sure if it was the paramedics or my offer of beer and steak but just as they were putting him inside the ambulance he grasped my hand tight and cracked a smile. That was a relief to see him smile and I knew he was gonna be alright.

After a week of observation I received a call that Frank was being released from the hospital and ready to be picked up. He looked weak and tired sitting in that wheel chair when I pulled up but by the time we made it home he was back to his old self and promptly reminded me that I owed him a beer. "Any time old man", I said. Without hesitation, "No time like the present", he replied. So at 10 o'clock on a beautiful Sunday morning we sat on the back porch drinking a beer with steaks on the grill and yes, there was a steak for Buddy. I'm a lot more patient with him now. I listen to him more and now he even gets his early morning weekend walks on time.

The Balloon

Molly Gast

Lady and I have been friends since I was ten years old. I first saw her in a pet shop after a summer ballet performance, and although she wasn't the dog I wanted, there was a connection there that just drew me, my Mom and my brothers in. We had to have her. She was small and a bit sad looking, with one floppy ear and one ear that pointed up like it ought to, and large brown eyes. How could anyone say no to a face like that? Well, my Dad could.

Dad was not happy when we brought her home. He shouted at Mom that she brought the dog home when he specifically told her not to. He didn't want a pet, and he certainly didn't want a dog, but within two weeks Lady managed to convince him that having her around was a worthwhile venture. I think it was the balloon that finally convinced him.

As a puppy, Lady had loads of energy and would bound around the house with the toy of the moment, playing with whoever was available at the time. Dad was trying hard to resist her charms, but I could tell his wall of indifference and resent was starting to crumble. Then, my brother came home from school one day with a helium balloon, and wanted to see if it could make Lady fly. We carried the dog into the back yard where Mom and Dad were working in our small garden, and they turned to watch as Alex released the puppy into the air with the balloon tied to her collar. Lady only ended up falling a few feet into the grass, because even though she was a very small Chihuahua mix she was still too heavy for just one balloon. Alex and I filed this scientific finding away for later, and decided we would try again with more balloons - but Lady had become preoccupied.

Lady had noticed this creature flying above her and must have decided it had an ominous presence, because she spent the next hour running through the yard, barking and jumping at the balloon. Dad chased after her, cheering her on, encouraging her in her vain attempts to capture the flying beast. He would pull it down for her most obligingly, then let it go when she jumped - which sent her on another tear through the yard.

That night when we sat down for dinner, Lady followed us into the dining room and stared up at us with her large brown eyes. Up until now, Dad had ignored her when we ate and made sure that everyone knew that feeding the dog at the table was unacceptable. We followed this rule strictly because Dad had been having a hard enough time accepting Lady into the family - we didn't want to make things worse.

However, it was Dad who broke the rule. While we were telling Mom and Dad about our school day struggles, I saw Dad's hand slip under the table with a piece of meat between his fingers. Lady perked up her floppy ear, and scooted under the table to get it. Dad saw me watching him, and gave me a wink.

Ready for Action

Rob Forest

When I was twenty-five years old and a newly minted Ensign in the United States Coast Guard I was assigned as Administration Officer to the Coast Guard Group in Mayport, Florida. The Coast Guard Group consisted of a Command Center, piers for some medium sized Coast Guard Cutters, and a Search and Rescue Station. A Search and Rescue Station or SAR Station in the Coast Guard runs pretty much like a Fire Station. Crews are generally on 48 hour duty shifts and they train and work on maintenance of the boats.

When a boat is in trouble and "Mayday! Mayday! Mayday!" is heard over the VHF radios in the Command Center things get a little crazy. The radioman on watch will hit a button and a loud claxon would sound all over the base. The on-duty crew would drop whatever else they might be doing--eating, sleeping, working on an engine, doing physical fitness drills--and run to the dock to launch the ready boat.

It was always exhilarating to watch the teamwork as a crew of four would get the 41 foot UTB rescue boat underway in usually less than five minutes. Many distressed mariners owe their lives to the speed and professionalism of these young crews. I'd been at Mayport a few days when I noticed this older Australian Shepherd wandering around the base. The dog limped a little, looked old, but had that pleasant look the Australian's are known for. I asked someone who owned the dog and a Chief Petty Officer just smiled. "He's the station mascot."

"What?" I asked, puzzled.

"It's a tradition in the Guard, Sir. A lot of stations and even some cutters have mascots. They just live aboard and the crew takes care of them. Casrep has been here a long time."

"Casrep? You mean like a "Casualty Report", a CASREP?"

"Yes," the CPO explained. "You see, we have base property on both sides of the road, and Casrep just figures it's all his property. He's been hit three or four times crossing that road. He always seems to come out a little worse for wear, but he's still going."

"He's moving a little slow," I said.

The CPO laughed. "Just don't get in his way if the SAR alarm goes off."

When I got to work the next morning I passed Casrep. He was sound asleep by the main gate. He looked like he planned to spend the day there in the shade by some palm trees. The gate is all the way across the base from the boat docks and the SAR station. I'd previously asked the SAR station Officer in Charge if I could go out on a rescue call. He told me I could, as long as I made it to the 41 before they got underway. They couldn't wait if it was an urgent call.

I'd just settled in behind my desk when I heard the SAR claxon go off. It blared three times, and then over the loud-hailer the radioman's voice boomed across the base. "Now hear this! Vessel taking on water one mile North of Jacksonville Jetties! Three souls on board!"

By the time the first words were out of the radioman's mouth I was out the door and sprinting around the corner of the building. It took me about thirty seconds to get to the corner of the building. As I rounded the corner I heard the 41 foot UTB's engines fire up. I was about a hundred yards away from the dock and I could see the boat crew running towards the boat from the other direction where their office. The mechanic must have already been on the boat to get it started so fast. Then, out of the corner of my eye I saw Casrep. He was rocketing towards the boat at high speed. I could barely believe it. He was moving so fast he looked like a young dog. There was no sign of his limp. In amazement I watched as Casrep leaped from the edge of the pier and easily cleared the gunwale to land sure-footed on the deck of the 41.

I made it to the boat about 15 seconds behind the boat crew. The lines were already cast off and within seconds we were underway with lights flashing and a siren blaring. I was still putting on a life vest when I saw Casrep standing next to the Coxswain in the cabin of the boat. "Does he always go on rescues?" I asked. The Coxswain, a young man of about twenty who was in command of the rescue boat took one hand off the wheel and patted Casrep on the head as we plowed down the river towards the sinking boat. "He's never missed a SAR call since I've been here. We all get days off, but Casrep is always on duty."

Over the next three years while I was stationed at Mayport I watched Casrep run for the 41 every time the SAR call went off. He was an amazing dog, and although I haven't been back to Mayport in twelve years, I have a feeling that Casrep is still on duty. The Coast Guard's motto is Semper Paratus – Always Ready – Casrep lived Semper Paratus every day.

Lost

Carolyn Hanlin

It isn't possible for Macy to get much closer to us. Every step we take Macy is right behind or beside or in front. She's everywhere and we are inseparable.

Macy, or May May, as our two year old daughter calls her, is an Australian Terrier. Cute, small and full of energy. Both Macy and our daughter. Actually, overflowing with energy is more like it. It's no surprise that between our daughter's toys, Macy's toys and the two of them playing that our house is a disaster and quite noisy.

Saturday started out as any normal day. We were up early, had everyone dressed and out the door for Macy's regular morning walk.

Macy began to jump and flip as the nylon leash jingled and was pulled it off the hook. She knew that sound and exactly what it meant. Walk time!

We had our routine. We took the same path through the neighborhood each morning. We saw the same people and she did her business in the same spot. Everything was exactly the same until we saw the sign.

"LOST DOG" – If anyone sees Vito please call us. Reward Offered.

There was a picture of Vito, the black lab. We had never seen him before in our neighborhood, but our eyes were peeled throughout our walk.

Every rustle of leaves, dog barking in the distance, every movement in the shadows caught our attention. Unfortunately, we made it home without finding Vito.

When the leash came off Macy was back to following us around with every step. She'd take turns following me, then my wife and occasionally our daughter, but that usually ended up with Macy wearing dress up clothes.

We all were scurrying around the house, cleaning, putting away clothes, doing our Saturday morning chores. When we were all done my wife and I sat and reveled in the clean, quiet aftermath.

Wait...Quiet? Lily, our daughter was sitting right next to us, but where was Macy? Immediately we began looking around.

"Macy!", "Macy, Come!" we all yelled.

Nothing. My heart sank. Had she gotten out somehow? She never leaves our side.

I opened the back door and yelled for her. Our back yard is fenced in and Macy never strays far from the steps.

Nothing.
I came back inside and began calling her again. My wife and I exchanged glances and we both had the same feeling at the same time. We know what Vito's owners must be feeling.

As we stared at each other the faintest sound came from upstairs. The sound of scratching and whimpering.

I grabbed Lily and followed closely behind my wife as we tried to follow the sounds. We both called for Macy without a response. The sounds were close.

Standing outside of our closet we both turned to each other again and smiled. We finally out paced Macy. With all of the running around and cleaning the house she just couldn't keep up.

After I had quickly hung our dry cleaning in the closet I shut the door, not realizing that Macy was still inside. In a flash I was downstairs vacuuming, never realizing she wasn't close behind.

Macy bust out of the closet as we opened the door. It was like she hadn't seen us in days. She quickly jumped into my wife's arms and began kissing her.

Fortunately, Macy was not lost.

We never did find out what happened to Vito, but the next day the sign was down.

Hopefully Vito was only locked in a closet by accident too.

Emily

Corrine Pastore

Growing up we had always had dogs. Little, miniature Poodles to be exact. They were fun, and they were quite spoiled. Mom and Dad both loved them and they received just as much attention as their real children. As we grew older, the dogs were replaced by visiting grandchildren and family. I believe Mom and Dad enjoyed the peace and quiet after all of those years and they enjoyed their time together.

Each time our family visited Mom and Dad they would be sitting in their chairs in the living room going about their normal business - Mom would be crocheting, Dad reading the paper. The television quietly on in the background. Mom's chair was right next to Dad's, just an arm's reach away. Dad would often, instinctively and lovingly, reach over and touch Mom's arm, just for a moment. Their love for each other was pure. Sometimes I felt like I was watching one of those shows from the fifties and sixties that portrayed the perfect family. That love spilled over to their children and grandchildren.

After Mom passed away everything changed. Their house was quiet. Dad was lost in himself. He rarely wanted visitors, to go out and visit or even interact with anyone. Dad sat alone in his chair and kept Mom's chair off limits. He would often snap at us or shoe us away if we tried to sit in her chair. We all knew it was difficult for him. They had been married for almost 56 years. We realized we needed to do something to help him along.

Several months passed and we decided that we needed to help Dad enjoy life again. It's what Mom would have wanted. As my sister and I bounced around ideas of support and hobbyist groups, we came to the realization that Dad needed company.

Emily was cute and petite. Her white curly hair blew in the breeze and her grey, playful eyes absolutely melted anyone that looked at them. At just over 8 pounds, we hoped that Emily, the Bishon Frise, would be the perfect match for Dad.

Unfortunately Emily had just lost her owner, an older woman, and she was now temporarily staying with her owners son and family. The son explained that since his Mom's passing Emily has seemed sad and was snapping at the smaller children. The family had toddlers and a small dog just wouldn't work out in their house. The son explain that they decided to put Emily up for adoption and hoped to find someone that would love her as much as his Mom did and give her a fun, safe home.

Dad and Emily met at Dad's house with much hesitation. Emily was a bit skittish and Dad was convinced he had little time or patience for a dog. It seemed to all change as Emily rounded the corner to find Dad sitting in his chair.

We saw a smile on Dad's face that we hadn't seen in the 8 months since Mom's passing and Emily didn't seem to have the same sadness we saw just a few days earlier. The two greeted each other as if they were old friends and I couldn't help but smile.

The two played together and smothered each other with kisses. It seemed to be the perfect match. Emily followed Dad as we moved from the living room to the kitchen like his new best friend.

Dad and I talked and reminisced about the Poodles we had when growing up and just how much Mom and Dad both loved them. Emily sat and listened tentatively at his feet.

"Honey, I really appreciate what you're trying to do, but I'm just not sure this is going to work out." Dad said.

"But Dad, you two need each other, you are a perfect fit to keep each other company."

Dad kept giving me reasons why he couldn't do it. My heart sank and I felt terrible for both of them, there was nothing I was going to do, or say, that was going to convince him otherwise.

"I'm sorry, as cute as she is..." Dad looked down at his feet as if to motion to Emily and realized that she was no longer sitting there.

"You see? She's more interested in exploring the house than sitting here with us." Dad said as he glanced around the kitchen. Emily was nowhere in sight.

I could hear the frustration in his voice. It was time to take Emily back and leave Dad. I tried, but without much luck. At least I had gotten him to smile, if only for a bit.

Dad walked back into the living room to take his usual position in his chair.

"Well, will you look at this!" Dad's voice carried from the next room.

I could only imagine what Dad was griping about now. I turned the corner to see Emily, curled in a tiny little ball, sleeping in Mom's chair. Dad was sitting in his, just an arm's reach away.

It's now been 3 years since Emily and Dad first met. Their new found love going strong. Each giving the other something they lost, companionship and love.

Thunder and Smiling

Gwen Slater

It's one of the worst sensations I had experienced. Everything around me shook and rumbled. As I sat there in complete darkness, forgetting where I was, how I had gotten there, I heard the jingling getting closer and it was approaching quickly.

A quick flash of lightening brought me back to reality, and now more rumbling. Suddenly there he was, standing above me on the bed, trying desperately to get as close to me as possible. Instinctively I screamed, but that only made things worse. His hot breath panting on my face. Duke was petrified.

A hefty eighty pounds of Golden Retriever had bolted from his bed and made his way in the dark to my room. Now he made every attempt to get next to me under the covers. I had only had Duke for a month before I learned just how scared of thunderstorms he really was. They warned me at the shelter of his anxiety, but now I had gotten to witness it first hand.

Eventually the storm passed and Duke calmed down, but it was a long night for both of us.

The next morning we both acted like nothing happened that night. We spent the morning preparing for our training. Duke was being trained as an Emotional Support Animal and I was being trained as his handler. It was something I had always wanted to do, work with animals and help others. Once my friends and family had met Duke and seen his calm and soothing demeanor they suggested we look into the training.

Up to this point Duke was perfect for the job. He was always extremely calm, gentle and friendly. He almost appeared to be smiling when he met new people and they were always eager to make them happy.

After the storm episode I grew concerned that he may not be a good fit after all. I had repeatedly checked with other trainers and groups that had experience in this area. They all told me that his storm anxiety could eventually be overcome and shouldn't hinder him, or us, from continuing our training track. So we pressed on.

Several months had passed as did a few storms. None as severe as our first encounter. As the thunder rumbled I did my best to show Duke there was nothing to fear. I was told that by not engaging him and acting calm he would learn that everything would be alright. It seemed to be working.

As the Summer months drew to a close we had already racked up quite a few visits to local homes, children's hospital's and fund raisers. Everyone loved to see Duke. His happiness seemed be contagious, especially to children. Both Duke and I enjoyed visiting children the best.

Today was a hot, humid and rainy Summer day and we had a late afternoon visit scheduled for a local children's ward. Exactly what we both enjoyed.

We quickly made our way inside, dried off and began making our rounds. Children laughing and smiling. Parents enjoying the happiness Duke was able to bring to their kids amidst the unfortunate situations.

About midway through our visit I heard it. The faint rumble of thunder. I became nervous and a bit anxious. My first instinct was to try and wrap things up before the storm was here full force, but I didn't want to disappoint anyone. I remained calm. Both for Duke and myself.

The rumbles got closer, the lightening brighter. As Duke sat next to one small child the lightening and thunder crashed simultaneously. It was close. The little girl, startled by the storm, immediately lost her smile. You could see the fear in her eyes as she tensed up and look around the room.

Just as quickly as the lightening flashed Duke gently flipped his head under her hand popping it up in a funny way. Her hand landed right on top of Dukes' head prompting an immediate giggle. The girl smiled again and began petting Duke. I caught a quick glance from Duke and his quirky little smile as if to tell me everything was going to be alright.

Share Your Stories

I hope you enjoyed these short stories. I'm always looking to hear from readers and everyone that has a great story to share.

Please visit the Stories of Tails website for updates and additional stories. **http://storiesoftails.com**

I hope to be able to include your story in the next series of short stories!

Remember, love your dog!

Chandler Jeffries

Please Leave a Review

I'd love to hear your thoughts on these short stories. Please share your experience and opinion in the customer reviews of this book located **here**.

Discover Other Books by Chandler Jeffries and Bella Media Publishing

14 Days to a Well-Bahaved Dog – The ultimate dog training book that can have your dog trained within the first few minutes of using these techniques.

Made in the USA
Las Vegas, NV
23 January 2021

16463385R00026